Sleepy
and
Busy
Animals

Mark Carwardine

**Illustrated by Martin Camm
and Dick Twinney**

Cover illustrations: a mouse lemur and a Japanese macaque

ISBN 1-899-762-23-X

This edition first published 1997 by
Horus Editions Limited, 1st Floor,
27 Longford Street, London NW1 3DZ

Printed in Singapore

Contents

The Mouse Lemur

The mouse lemur is a sleepy animal.

It spends several months of the year resting or hibernating in a hollow tree. While hibernating it eats hardly anything and goes completely stiff. This mouse lemur is fast asleep.

Mouse lemurs live in the jungles of Madagascar, spending most of their

time high in the trees. At night, when feeding, they often call out to other mouse lemurs in the darkness.

The Raccoon

The raccoon is a busy animal.

It is always getting into trouble and is probably the most mischievous animal in the world.

Raccoons like to live near people and will make their homes almost anywhere. Active mostly at night, they spend the daytime sleeping in a hollow

tree, or in an attic or garden shed.
    These cheeky raccoons are looking
for scraps inside an overturned dustbin.

The Dormouse

The dormouse is a sleepy animal.

It curls up into a tiny ball of fur and spends the winter fast asleep. It may sleep for as long as seven months, safely hidden under a pile of leaves. It is very fat, stuffed with all the food it collected during the autumn. This dormouse looks very comfortable inside its special nest.

The Macaque

The macaque is a busy animal.

It is a kind of monkey, but is like people in many ways. It learns quickly and can teach other macaques tricks. It can even walk about on two legs.

The Japanese macaque lives high up in the freezing cold mountains of Japan. During very bad winters, it has to keep

itself warm by
taking hot baths in
the warm water
from volcanic springs.

   This Japanese macaque
is carrying sweet
potatoes in its arms. It
is going to dip them in
the sea because, just like
some people, it likes the
salty taste.

The Koala

The koala is a sleepy animal.

It spends as many as eighteen hours every day dozing or sleeping. It is active for only a few hours during the middle of the night, when it eats as many leaves as possible, before going back to sleep again.

Koalas look just like small bears. But

they are
related to
kangaroos,
and female
koalas even
have pouches on
their bellies.
  This koala is fast
asleep in the fork of
a tree, high above
the ground.

The Water Shrew

The water shrew is a busy animal.

It only lives for about one and a half years. With such a short life, it always seems to be in a hurry and rarely finds time to sleep or rest.

Water shrews are active at night and during the day, busily searching for fish, frogs, insects, and other animals to eat.

This water shrew is swimming to the bottom of a pond, where it can stay for about twenty seconds before floating back up to the surface.

The Bear

The bear is a sleepy animal.

It sleeps during the winter in a cave or under a dead tree. But sometimes, when the weather is nice and warm, it may wake up and wander outside for a while.
   Black bears like to eat fruit, berries, nuts, insects, and a variety of other food. But their favourite food is honey.

This black bear is curling up ready to go to sleep after eating some honey. It is surrounded by angry bees because the honey was taken from their hive.

The Orang-utan

The orang-utan is a busy animal.

It gets up very early in the morning and then spends the rest of the day searching for fruit, leaves, and other tasty morsels to eat. It can often be seen in a jungle, swinging from branch to branch, high up in the trees.

Orang-utans have very long arms.

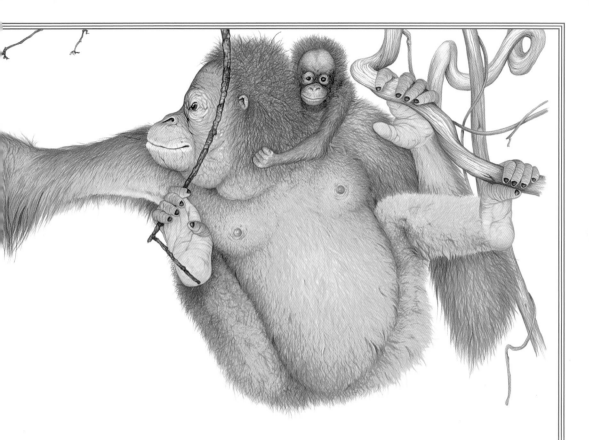

In fact, their arms are so long that when
they stand upright their fingers almost
touch the ground. This orang-utan and
her baby are collecting figs.

The Hamster

The hamster is a sleepy animal.

It goes to sleep in the autumn, inside its underground burrow, and does not go outside again until the following spring.

This hamster is using its cheeks like shopping baskets, to carry food back to its burrow. It is storing seeds, shoots, and roots to help it survive the winter.

Golden hamsters are popular pets, but they are also common animals in the wild, in parts of Europe and Asia. They live along riverbanks, in fields and deserts, and on mountain slopes.

The Pine Marten

The pine marten is a busy animal.

It looks more like a giant squirrel as it races around in the trees. But it belongs to a different family of animals, called the mustelids. Its closest relatives are otters, badgers, and ferrets.

Pine martens are active at night and during the day. They eat many different

animals, including mice, small birds, and caterpillars. This pine marten has caught a squirrel to eat for its supper.

Glossary

hibernation a long sleep or time for keeping still during very cold or bad weather

Madagascar a large island off the south-eastern coast of Africa, in the Indian Ocean

morsel a small bite or little piece of food

mustelid an animal that is in the same family as badgers, stoats, skunks, and weasels

pouch a small bag or sack. A female koala keeps her baby safe in a soft pouch on her belly.

spring a flow of water from the ground. Warm or hot water comes out of a volcanic spring.

Index